Sea Lions

Kate Riggs

seedlings

CREATIVE EDUCATION • CREATIVE PAPERBACKS

Published by Creative Education and Creative Paperbacks
P.O. Box 227, Mankato, Minnesota 56002
Creative Education and Creative Paperbacks are
imprints of The Creative Company
www.thecreativecompany.us

Design by Ellen Huber
Production by Chelsey Luther
Printed in the United States of America

Photographs by Dreamstime (Jens Hilberger, Hugoht, Izanbar,
Bob Suir), Shutterstock (Eric Isselee), SuperStock (BlueGreen
Pictures, imagebroker.net, Minden Pictures, NaturePL, NHPA)

Library of Congress Cataloging-in-Publication Data
Riggs, Kate.
Sea lions / Kate Riggs.
p. cm. — (Seedlings)
Summary: A kindergarten-level introduction to sea lions,
covering their growth process, behaviors, the oceans they
call home, and such defining features as their whiskers.
Includes index.
ISBN 978-1-60818-516-0 (hardcover)
ISBN 978-1-62832-116-6 (pbk)
1. Sea lions—Juvenile literature. 2. Adaptation (Biology)
—Juvenile literature. I. Title. II. Series: Seedlings.

QL737.P63R544 2014
599.79'75—dc23   2013051259

CCSS: RI.K.1, 2, 3, 4, 5, 6, 7;
RI.1.1, 2, 3, 4, 5, 6, 7; RF.K.1, 3; RF.1.1

First Edition
9 8 7 6 5 4 3 2 1

TABLE OF CONTENTS

Hello, sea lions!

Sea lions are ocean animals.

They have
flippers
for feet.

Sea lions have long, furry bodies.

They have whiskers on their faces.

Sea lions have flat noses. Ear flaps stick out from their heads.

Sea lions are meat eaters.

They catch fish.

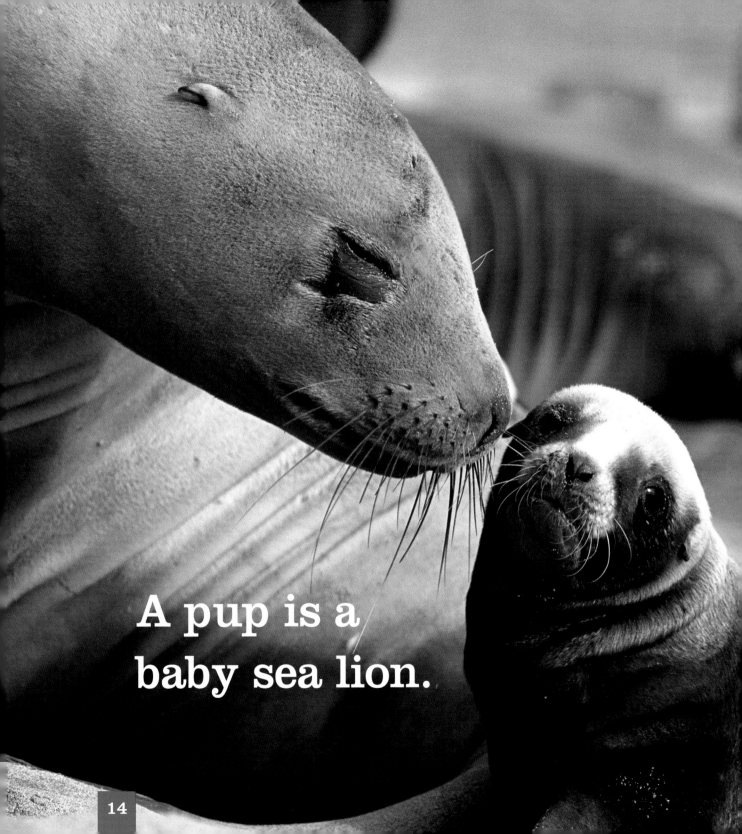

A pup is a
baby sea lion.

Pups live with their mother on a beach. A group of sea lions on land is called a colony.

Sea lions swim
and swim.

They rest on a beach.

Goodbye,

sea lions!

Picture a Sea Lion

nose

whiskers

hind flipper

snout

eye

ear flap

fur

neck

foreflipper

21

furry: describing the short, hairy coat of an animal

ocean: a big area of deep, salty water

Read More

Sexton, Colleen. *Sea Lions.*
Minneapolis: Bellwether Media, 2008.

Shively, Julie. *Baby Sea Lion.*
Nashville, Tenn.: CandyCane Press, 2005.

Websites

San Diego Zoo Animal Cams & Videos
http://kids.sandiegozoo.org/animal-cams-videos
Click on the picture of a California sea lion to watch a video.

Sea Lions Coloring Pages
http://www.supercoloring.com/pages/category/mammals
/sea-lions/
Print out pictures of sea lions to color.

Index